T0290806

more praise for
LOSS AND OTHER RIVERS THAT DEVOUR

" 'I hate myself because I cannot write this' is a line from Gustavo Barahona-Lopez's book that reveals the collection's courage to confront with uncompromising honesty, and that marks so many poems that help us to love our colonized selves better. Through poems that look into the complex feelings of mourning, resent, disorientation, and colonial violences like machiste, these poems bloom past the myth of unemotional self to a foundation that we struggle to find, because we never lost it, but must believe in and form now. Language heals here. It reconstitutes our reality. I read this collection with my mom, and an understanding and recognition of ourselves became palpable, and we cried, but now, we too are reaching for blood—or rather, understand ourselves through the speaker as 'a place reaching for its foundation.' "

Sara Borjas
author of *Heart Like a Window, Mouth Like a Cliff*

"Look down through the waters of memory, separation, grieving, and loss and you will see a village in which someone called your true name sweetly and some other, who was your father, still walks with an imagined you that is a ghost. In this book, Barahona-López takes us through our own bodies, sifts the waters, both sweet and salt, in an intimate invitation, one of longing and brokenness. He crafts a mythic and otherworldly tenderness, fearless in his adoption of forms like the elegy, the ode, the couplet. Who has not experienced relational rupture? Whole poems I imagine sung out from many lips in kinship and claimed, written on their bodies, because they seem already to be an extension of the indelible inking, a scarring of the body and a stitching over as he guides us towards a healing, always a process of becoming. Flutter the eyes against the falling rain or the falling water we make. This is a book that calls one to shed artifice and shields and walls, both internal and external, political and familial. And it is absolutely necessary right now. Right now."

Raina J. León, PhD
author of *profeta without refuge*

" 'Father told me I should never cry./ What a thing to demand of a waterfall,' Gustavo Barahona-López writes. If you've ever known what it feels like to be the son of a Mexican immigrant father, this book is for you. And if you haven't, this book is especially for you. Here is a guide on how to find opportunity beyond barren deserts, on how some men carve dreams from the bones of their tender children. What becomes of masculinity after you've weeped into your father's arms? Who do you pray to if you cannot speak to the 'Purépecha gods [because you] do not know their names'? This poet ruminates deeply while running from himself until his body aches, then builds a home from his accumulated pain. These poems are moments of catharsis, of individual suffering turned collective understanding. These notes are a mourning over our future; they are a young man's concerns about not only his survival, but that of his own hijos. I want to live more fully after reading *LOSS AND OTHER RIVERS THAT DEVOUR*. I want to joke with everyone around me, and embrace our endless destinies. I want to reread these poems beside my father, Ignacio, somewhere beneath the California sky, until the language becomes our dust. 'Mis hijos/ forgive me for what/ I drowned.' Barahona-López has offered us a window into machismo and anti-machismo; into Mexican fatherhood and the lineage of childhood that follows; into fighting for your place in this devouring world, all at once.' "

Alan Chazaro

author of *Piñata Theory*
and *This Is Not a Frank Ocean Cover Album*

NOMADIC PRESS

OAKLAND

111 FAIRMONT AVENUE
OAKLAND, CA 94611

BROOKLYN

475 KENT AVENUE #302
BROOKLYN, NY 11249

WWW.NOMADICPRESS.ORG

MASTHEAD

FOUNDING PUBLISHER
J. K. FOWLER

ASSOCIATE EDITOR
MICHAELA MULLIN

EDITOR
RAINA J. LEÓN

DESIGN
JEVOHN TYLER NEWSOME

MISSION STATEMENT

Through publications, events, and active community participation, Nomadic Press collectively weaves together platforms for intentionally marginalized voices to take their rightful place within the world of the written and spoken word. Through our limited means, we are simply attempting to help right the centuries' old violence and silencing that should never have occurred in the first place and build alliances and community partnerships with others who share a collective vision for a future far better than today.

INVITATIONS

Nomadic Press wholeheartedly accepts invitations to read your work during our open reading period every year. To learn more or to extend an invitation, please visit: www.nomadicpress.org/invitations

DISTRIBUTION

Orders by teachers, libraries, trade bookstores, or wholesalers:

Nomadic Press Distribution
orders@nomadicpress.org
(510) 500-5162
nomadicpress.org/store

Small Press Distribution
spd@spdbooks.org
(510) 524-1668 / (800) 869-7553

Loss and Other Rivers That Devour
© 2022 by Gustavo Barahona-López

This book was made possible by a loving community of chosen family and friends, old and new.

For author questions or to book a reading at your bookstore, university/school, or alternative establishment, please send an email to info@nomadicpress.org.

Cover art: Arthur Johnstone

Published by Nomadic Press, 111 Fairmount Avenue, Oakland, California 94611

First printing, 2022

Library of Congress Cataloging-in-Publication Data

Title: *Loss and Other Rivers That Devour*
p. cm.
Summary: *Loss and Other Rivers That Devour* charts the evolution of one son's grief as he reconciles his identity with the expectations of his late father. In this journey of becoming, Gustavo Barahona-López struggles with and is shaped by loss and its many hauntings: toxic masculinity, colonial erasures of language and heritage, and the legacy of the United States' xenophobic immigration policies.

[POETRY / Subjects & Themes / Family. 2. POETRY / American / Hispanic & Latino. 3. POETRY / American / Colonialism. 4. POETRY / General.] I. III. Title.

LIBRARY OF CONGRESS CONTROL NUMBER: 2021949454

ISBN: 978-1-955239-19-6

LOSS AND OTHER RIVERS THAT DEVOUR

GUSTAVO
BARAHONA-LÓPEZ

LOSS AND OTHER RIVERS THAT DEVOUR

GUSTAVO
BARAHONA-LÓPEZ

**NOMADIC
PRESS**

CONTENTS

introduction

reading guide

INTRODUCTION

This collection centers on my ever-evolving grief for the death of my father, Adolfo López. He was a gifted storyteller. I could spend hours listening to his tall tales about escaping deadly whirlpools and beating men twice his size. He no doubt influenced my desire to become a writer. My father never showed his vulnerability if he could help it. Raised in rural México, he believed that men must be strong and show no fear in the face of adversity. Further he considered himself the patriarch of my family and expected my mother, siblings, and I to obey him without question. After his cancer diagnosis, whenever I'd ask--"are you afraid of dying?"--he'd insist that he was not afraid and was ready for God to take him if God needed him. Only once did I crack through his stoic masculinity. When I read him a poem I wrote about his pancreatic cancer and my fear of losing him, I lost it and started crying halfway through reading the poem. To my surprise he began crying with me. We grieved the years we'd never get to share.

After his death in 2007 I was primed to become the 'man of the family', but rejected the role knowing that I didn't fit the mold. As I grew into adulthood and eventually fatherhood, I began to question the lessons on masculinity he imparted. I didn't want to rule my family with

an iron fist. Instead I reflected on witnessing the impact of my father's rage on my family. As a child, I feared my own anger and I trained myself to be a quiet person. As I work to undo the socialization I received from my father, my grief for my father shifts continuously. I know now that the loss of my father will never cease to carry me in its currents.

The poems you are about to read are an incomplete cartography of my growth, my setbacks, my longing, and my mourning.

Welcome to my rivers.

BUILT TO MOURN

Sometimes I convince   myself
                              I was built   to mourn
          programmed   by mitochondrial
     DNA   or perhaps   conditioned   by scarcity

          I mourn the past   the chances
     not taken   the healing   postponed
parental sacrifices   to unmeritocratic gods
               subjugation of   my ancestors

                              by my ancestors
               my blood   strangles itself
          my dead   and yours

I mourn the present   inability to stay
          in this moment   here
               the children murdered   here
the nation   -less   can populate   their own   planet
          wilting bookstores   artesanía shops
     news as myth-making   with no protagonist
          systems are   the only demi-gods
               emperor penguins   collapse into

                                                    our inequity

I mourn the future   humanity
                              as self-destructive
                    sinking cities
                              commodified   filtered tears

        my life   as fiction
                    the earth   wants
                         to forget   but scabs
persist

        mis hijos   mis hijos   mis hijos
                    forgive me   for what
                         I drowned

KALLIO, THE SUNKEN VILLAGE

I walk into a ghost village.
> Water half lives in buildings

that once recorded
> the transitory. You see,
>> for all its movement,
>> even a man-made

lake holds onto eternity
> like it is a coin begging to be flipped.

I stare in emerald waves
> swaddle piles of stones
>> that perhaps once made a wall,
> perhaps a home. Now
>> a rearticulated sand.

> At what point does a lake
>> cease to be
>>> artificial?
>> When is it purely body?
> The permanent
> recalls a launch
>> into itself.
> Cerulean cloud

chastens me.

I make out sets of five petals
surrounding a golden halo.

        I bite my tongue.

                Atonement made tangible.

    My blood outgrows my body,
becomes water.

        It spatters on green rock,

            disappears. How do I

                        taste? I wonder

            why so many gods

                chose to make us out of clay,

        mud to be breathed

            into being. After all,

                even stones have a half-life.

WATERFALL DUPLEX

Father told me I should never cry.
What a thing to demand of a waterfall.

> I cannot ask more of myself, a waterfall.
> He tells me he almost drowned in a lake.

Whirlpool nearly drowned him in a lake.
Part of my father resides in the water.

> I've learned to reside in my own water.
> Shutting out light reminds me of home.

Father kept out the sunlight at home.
Who, I wonder, was he hiding from?

> I can't name the fears I am hiding from.
> Father spits blood into a plastic cup.

Writing a poem, I give him his bloody cup.
I recite my poem. We both begin to cry.

CONVIVIR DOES NOT MEAN TO LIVE TOGETHER

It means to break bread juntos.
To form comunidad. To be present,
beyond the first of the month
or when you remind people
to wash their own damn platos.
GOOOAAALLL!!! in English is a weak statement.
In Spanish, ¡¡¡¡¡¡GOOOOOOOOOOOOOOOLLL!!!!!!
is an experience.
En español, love has gradations. Te quiero pero no te amo,
says a teenage boy trying to have it both ways.
La güera is your light-skinned prima.
El gringo is that white man
who mispronounces two phrases in español
and expects to be praised like he recited
a García Lorca poem by heart.

Mojado is an immigrant who survives
coyotes, la migra y ese maldito río.
Deserves a towel, chocolate, and a fireplace
to take the chill from the bones.
Aunque ahora es el desierto que toma
el agua, la piel y los sueños de los migrantes.

I used to visit México for months at a time:
play canicas, scale cerros,
eat mangos and pepinos with chile and limón.
Español invadía mi cuerpo como susurro
diciendo, "I am the adopted, the imposed,
the forgotten."

Cuando se me caía la mollera, the curandera
did not massage me, me sobaba.
She would draw espiritus from me with an egg,
rub the huevo against me like an elegy to syncretism,
to Purépecha gods I can never pray to.
I do not know their names.

The times my monolingual father called me a pendejo,
it hurt worse than all the English curse words
I learned in elementary school combined.
When the word pendejo leaves the lips of my papá,
it means I am a failure y nunca seré nada.
¿Cómo se dice therapy en español?

I no longer dream in Spanish.

My nightmares are in English.
But when I cry o doy mi corazón,
lo hago en two different tongues.

MI PADRE, EL MÁS FUERTE DEL MUNDO

Mi padre trabajó desde los cinco años
Trabajó para mantener a sus hermanos
Sobrevivió lo más duro de la vida
Cruzó al país de oportunidad
Se casó con una de sus muchas seguidoras
Con mi mamá
Trabajó para asegurar nuestro futuro
Quedó deshabilitado en el trabajo

Mi padre es una indomable fuerza
Con un poder infinito
Con una mente de genio
Lo único que le faltó fue oportunidad
Que este país no le brindo,
Pero que ahora me brinda a mí

Aunque estaba deshabilitado
Podía noquear a cualquiera
Hasta al mismo Julio César Chávez
Yo trato de describir su grandeza
Pero no creo que sea posible hacerlo
Pero este es un esfuerzo

Nací idéntico

Su reencarnación en vida

Un clon

Un hermano gemelo

Menor por tan solo unas décadas

Los mismos ojos, el mismo pelo

La misma mente

El mismo amor por la familia

Pudo haber sido grande

Pudo haber sido casi un Dios

En ojos estadounidenses

Pero tuvo que trabajar por su familia amada

Padre, mi guía-Padre, mi Dios

Lo amamos por ello

95 por ciento cáncer, páncreas

Hijo de Dios

Seguidor bendito

Se me va porque es necesitado en lo más alto del cielo

Se me va porque lo necesita Dios

HOW TO MAKE A MAN

At conception, conjure
the masculine with will.
Declare, *My son*
was the biggest
baby born at the hospital
today.

Close the blinds
of your home, mistrust
burrows like screw-
worms into flesh.

Tell your son
he is useless
just enough for him
to believe. Turn
his skin to leather.
An artisan, you
crosshatch soft hands.

Destabilize his world
like a blown

tire, rim sparks
on asphalt, leaves a trail
of wildfires.

Compose him
stories. Build entire worlds.
Myth: *I once beat a gym
rat for talking shit. Jacked
abs didn't save the bastard
from my fist.*

Instruct: *Restrain manhood
like a fish. Put your thumb inside
its mouth. Let it bite
down, draw blood.
Repeat.*

Refuse to look him
in the face when he threatens
to cry. After all
you learned to swim
by being thrown.

Ask your son, How
many girls are you dating?
When you know
the answer. Then
remind him of how you
had three girlfriends
in two countries.

And one night
when you've had too
many beers,
apologize
for what we
have become.

GREEN, HOW I WANT YOU

My father once raised plants for a living
He carried flower beds
Carnations, lilacs, peonies
Water, fertilizer, dirt
The flower beds broke him
The carrying cracked his spinal chord
The flowers swallowed the tender in him
Drank the dancing in him

❀   ❀   ❀

My mother fell in love
With my father dancing
She has a green thumb
Planting is her fertilizer
Blooming her joy
My father threw her blooming
Onto concrete
Cracked pots, broken roots
His fingers around her neck
Like a vine, so green, so green

＊　　　＊　　　＊

I sprouted without light
Without the carrying
There was so much blooming
The red, the fire, the thorn
The belt, the rod, the vitriol
My bruises bloomed green

＊　　　＊　　　＊

Vines embedded themselves
In my veins, roots snaked through
My capillaries until they broke skin
How do I call myself a garden?
Green, how I want you green
Every day a new leaf, a new sprout
Every day a small green death

.

I RUN FROM MYSELF AND MY BODY ACHES

I smash mirrors. No eye wear protects me from my crafting. I am adobe sun amalgamation, straw and dirt. Heat becomes itself on asphalt. Stomach rolls like a landscape. Angles are a national monument. My joints naturally begin to decompose. Family medical history hunts like a leopard. Consume the body as something to hide. With so much mutation why can't I be superhuman. Instead, scalpels are the paint brushes of my future. Body as calamity, as breathless canvas. I shorten my life with pleasures. Only mangled steel away from expiration. What if my cuts never healed? Would I slice myself like an invitation? I turn into desiring object desired, jagged shards gnawing at my reflection.

THE FACE OFF

My father stared Death in the face and
made him laugh

Afterward they went off together
for a drink

It was my father's first drink
in two Cancer years

TO DREAM IS TO MOURN

I.

The walls of the barn rot hungrily
Butcher hooks decorate
My body like lights
On a Christmas tree
Shallow light bounces off
My father's crutches
He seizes in primordial pain
Seeing me he lifts
Himself to his feet
Hugs a support beam
My father knows he will die
He falls to the ground
Spinal cord shatters
Flames birth flames
Scorch the darkness
I offer my broken body
My father is incandescent

Ⅱ.

A worn park bench sits
Cradles my father
And me on the shoreline
We look across emerald waves
Toward a man-made fiefdom
A thick layer of white feces claims
The island for the birds
Moldy bread brings the flock
Like a gentle poison
Frenzy ensues decisively,
My father snatches
A pigeon in rough hands
Pulls a pocket knife

I notice fishing line
Snaked around each crease
Of the pigeon's feet
Two completed amputations
Three in progress
I search the ground for pigeon toes
My father cuts and untangles
He shows me groves

Not unlike those that cover
His body
He lets the pigeon fly
My father staggers on his crutches

I go lucid

All my questions
Flock into my mind
I am not vessel
Enough to contain them
I open my mouth
Feathers, beaks, and claws gurgle
In my throat
I shut my mouth
Listen
My father
Does not know
He is dead

Ⅲ。
Atop a writhing sea a black
Granite base balances
There escalators point to nowhere
Run perpendicular

My father waits in his wheelchair
I sail to him on a raft
Around my neck is a chain,
An anchor for my vessel

Holographic doors open
I push my father into the sea
He rematerializes behind me
Won't let me touch him

He will not let me hold

RETROFITTING BRIDGES:
TALES OF A LOST SOUL IN THE THIRD SPACE

I came to you (myself) at a time of unmitigated confusion.
                              Wind and rain enveloped me like a
                              ghostly cloak.

I need you to love me even when you hate me.

My skin cracks   and ruptures
                    into heart-shaped snowflakes.

They shatter into sand, a dust as brittle as identity.

                                        I add love
                                        to insult.

                                        Stir in hate
                                        with a dash of
                                        consciousness
                                        and bake to perfection.

                                        I used to feed
                                        you mediocrity.

Now you revel at
being consumed
by a utopia that will
always remain
a potentiality.

I retrofit bridges
                    because my life depends on it.
My being is fused to the structures.

                              As I step onto them,
sections of concrete instantaneously
combust around me.

            I have lost count of the number of times
                        I have drowned trying to cross.

I am in a perennial state of healing myself and my bridges.
But I continue to do so.

I
hate
myself
because
I
cannot
write
this.

I am trapped in the

        in-between,

                but I am at home in this third-space

for it is the space where I was born, where I grew up, and where I
continue to live.

At this moment I am changing.
        My cells are dying and being reborn.
                My neurons cyclone trying to remember the
        sensation of being alive. I am

the shaman and the hexed.
        The witnessed and the invisible.

I am building an army.

I have drafted hundreds of thousands complete with

    heavy artillery,

        bullets, and
            grenades.

With this	my army of
letters	words
will	terrorize,
destroy	assumptions
I will	bombard.

You are not just you. You are a culmination of every book, limestone, conspiracy, oppression, empathy, and all else you have experienced. You have taken from every person just as you have given.

On this day I want you to know that I love you,

especially when I hate you.

LICENSE TO LIVE

In the warm, afternoon
light, the migrant tore
open an envelope,
and found a glistening
license, stamped with
the dancing letters,
D-M-V.
After he carefully placed
the laminated treasure
into his skinny
wallet, he grabbed
his keys and flew
into a car, barely a grade
above a jalopy.
Without the usual fear,
he let the vehicle roar.
After all, he was official.

But that was years ago
and the faded letters no longer danced,
and the card was expired.
At last, the migrant gave the license

to his son, who in turn put it
into a skinny wallet they purchased together
at a flea market.

The son, trying to remember
his father's face, often stared into
his father's laminated eyes.
The son pulled
at the memories trapped inside
the holographic image
the way we all long to recall
that someone that we have lost.

FOUNDATION

I.

November 18, 1993
I have seen Time Magazine's "The New Face
Of America" before. She is my sister
Or my cousin or that distant auntie.
The auntie that calls indígenas savages.
America is computer-generated familial,
Morphing to create the kind of offspring
That can eat the sun whole. Her eyes
Sing an egalitarian promise but
I know when she lies. The nation
Desires brown flesh only as long
As it remains theoretical, like a costume
It uses to scare itself in the mirror.
Rejected, I used to obsess over Aztec
Deities as if they could quell my hunger
For place. Mestizaje offered fortification
From empire with empire. But when I spoke
To my mother about Coatlicue, she
Could not see herself in the earth,
Prayed to the Virgen de Guadalupe instead.
If only my ancestors still talked to me.

Perhaps I would not be at the whim
Of reimagined nationhood.

II.

DNA test tries to tell me I am not who I imagined myself to be.
Percentage points are allotted to scattered kin who may or may not
know I exist. Continents pangea into one another like a collapsing
star. The gods I was supposed to worship dance upon my cartography.
The God I learned to worship becomes ink. Catholicism drips from
my map like a stain. I trace voyages along oceans, chart the trails that
allegedly led to my conception. I never take a DNA test.

III.

My past holds

    Too many secrets.

        I will never hear.

A story

    Of silences

     Subdued.

    Where do I come from?

A breath.

      A breaking.

A dream   Realized.

I am a place

    Reaching

       For its own foundation.

IV.

Please forgive me for forgetting

    That which I never witnessed,

Myths I was never told. I know

    I've been a bad son but

Remember I am but a pebble thrown

    Into the time river.

I can build a dam but not alone. I can

    Remake myself but not alone.

I will not speak for you. I haven't

    The right to. You do not know

Who I am, perhaps you know exactly

    Where I've been. I welcome you

Into the caverns within me. Be sure

    Not to get lost among the crystals.

I want to anchor my dream of a
        Decolonial somewhere
To your being. How can I know
        Something different without
Tracing something different? How
        Do I build from a corroded base?

V.

My three languages are colonized.

        Como serpientes me envuelven,

A patchwork of scales and skin.

        Me asusta la fuerza de mi voz,

My sharp words cause ruptures

        En nepantla pero esa palabra

Is not mine to claim, not mine.

        Quisiera tanto tener comunidad,

To know the original source

        Mi cultura pero nunca lo sabré.

I search inside my own becoming

        Busco mi pasado en lo que seré.

LETTER TO FUTURE SELF

Dearest me, do you still
Live? Is sunlight still a thing?

Is your cannibalism radioactive
Or still capitalist?

Are your body and your city submerged
Underwater? Crabs eat gourmet epidermis.

Is your society post-racial?
Just kidding, I know
It's not post-racial.

Have you learned to sit
Your mind still?

Do you still forget your
Dreams like dimes into a wishing well?

Does your body let you
Self-care? How broken

Is too broken? Are you still broken?
Are we?

I offer you my mistakes
Like handcuffs. Best forget

Yours, truly.

THERE IS A GHOST IN MY HOUSE

He does not make lights
flicker or move
objects or make noises
in the night.
He does not try to scare
people by appearing
at inopportune moments.
He lives and lets live.

He wonders what is
really behind the light
and when he should cross
into it. Likes to stream
"The Exorcist" on the family
Netflix account although demons
scare him and exorcisms
seem inconvenient.

He wishes his father had
not gotten cancer
and that they had shared

a proper goodbye
before each became a ghost
of what they had once been.
Curse family
histories. A father,
son, and holy
spirit gone.

I have a ghost
in my house
but I don't want him
to leave because right
now things are
safe and familiar.
He feels empty,
transparent
and so I am afraid
that I will lose
him again.

ELEGY FOR JAKELIN

7-year-old Guatemalan girl who died in Border Patrol custody is identified ...

Each day I open class with a morning circle.
Nineteen 7- and 8-year-olds sit
on a colorful rug. Talk about
their favorite color,
ideal superpowers, how they feel
or who they will be when they grow up.
I tell them I wish I could teleport. Cross
walls without a second thought. Be
one blink away from my family.
At recess I read about a 7-year-old
who died in Border Patrol custody
after navigating the New Mexican desert.
Her name is Jakelin Caal Maquin.
I begin to wonder:
Did she make walking through the desert a game?
Count the number of cacti. Make
messages with stones in the sand.
I wonder if she went to school.
Did she have to leave midway
through the year to work
picking strawberries
or donkey dung to sell

like my father?
I imagine my classroom with 20 students.
Would she color in desert sunrises?
Or would the deep sunset reds and oranges
be her inspiration. I wonder
if she knew where she was going.
What was America to her? I wonder
if she spoke K'iche' or English or Spanish or Mam.
What would she write about?
One of my students wrote,
Another word for ordinary is God.
I prep the math Do Now on the white board.
My students are learning multiplication.
I wonder if she knew her times tables.
What is 15,000 children times two parents
in a different detention facility?
My students know any number of bottles of water
times Border Patrol boots equals zero.
Did she know the definition of terror,
or did she call it fear?
The not knowing tears.

BOND

Once,   you broke my earth   open.
   Brought down my constellations   with a slingshot,
      Planted seeds in   the nape of my neck,
Poured spirit   down my throat.

With you,   I sing new stars into being.
      I nourish saplings into   forests spanning my back.
        I drink of you   like a communion.
  With me, you let your fire burn incandescent.

    You blast dams leaving nascent   waterfalls in your wake.
You remember you are enough.
         Once, you rip me open.
    You make me roll up my skin   (scars and all)

Like the poster   for a movie you would never
    Watch.   You make me leave   myself behind
  Like a carcass scavenged clean by your need
   Of me.   Do you love me enough not to

     Kill me?   Is that your way of letting go?
I tear you to shreds once

Maybe twice   or three times.   I watch
        You through the prism of   my own cuts.   Resist

The urge   to collect your ribbons   and make you
        Whole again.   I tell you your smile   is the cruelest
Of promises.   I berate you   with my silence.
But once I speak,   I mend us.   Or maybe

You do the mending   this time.   Out of this thread
              We make our specters.

THEY CALL US FENCE-HOPPERS, WE CALL OURSELVES SKYWALKERS

We began to incubate our wings to reach
the sun. Before any tea parties or unifications,
before the first fingers curled around a flag pole.
We practiced collecting mangoes with no ladders,
climbed smoke to harvest pearls from the sky.
Each night we delighted in picking cobwebs
out of each other's hair.

Now, the gateway to the earth, the heavens
is ajar to us. We drink water with our eyes.
Rivers will never devour us.
Joining hands, we synchronize
our flight patterns. Rocket
towards the moon like Apollo.

They call us locusts forgetting
how we have fed them.
Our drums are their thunder,
our sabotage is their sublime.
Their failure is not our responsibility,
yet we reach out to them still.

Our children use walls as volleyball nets,
switch sides at each half.
Our children project themselves upon
deserts, pouring smiles down as if the cacti
held cameras in the sheer of their needles.
We play hide and seek among the clouds,
sculpt them into phoenix feathers. We chase
each other over mountains and into valleys
knowing we chose when to return to the earth.
el agua

HOME, A BECOMING

I remind myself that my legs are countries. The way
Borders are the hemlines of worn jeans.

How do you say goodbye to backyard pomegranates?
They demand remittances like body parts.

Lips and arms and cheeks to be kissed by a monarch
Butterfly. I rip off the barbed wire across my spine,

Protection for the casa triste that lives on my temple.
How do you greet America? Like a lost lover

Torn from you by time or lust or hate?
Like a child not at peace with self?

I become the orchard and the railroad. I raise
The children, bury the dead. I make myself

A home. I build connection like water creates
Caverns, writing names on stone walls.

CROWS HOLD GRUDGES
FOR GENERATIONS

Some days I wonder what crows
squawk about, what it'd be like
to caress their dark
feathers like a bouquet
of baby's breath.
I think they are talking shit
about me.
How my hair is not black,
like I deceived
myself into believing,
but dark brown.
Brown as in body
breached.
Body as in wings
severed. My wings
are marinated in buffalo
sauce, teeth nibble on the
cartilage while tongue extracts
morsels between bones.
I fear my ancestors
will not recognize me.
How many languages have I lost?

I, of the impoverished lexicon,
watch words pop
like bubbles after kissing
blades of grass. I am
much too fractured
to believe in bygones.
I am too much earth to die.

READING GUIDE

Theme: **Identity**

Identity is often a fraught process in which the specific content of people's lives are contextualized within the larger social world which may not be hospitable to them or their experiences. Consider these questions: What communities do you belong to? Which of your identities are most present in your daily life? How do your identities impact your decisions and how you interact with others?

Prompt
1. Using cut out pictures from magazines create a collage that shows who you are. Then, write about why you selected those images and how they represent you.

2. Write a letter to an ancestor in the broad sense that includes at least 3 questions. This can be someone who is related to you, like a great-grandparent, or someone from

the past that you feel a connection to (in my case Pablo Neruda or Octavia Butler).

3. Make a list of as many of your identities as possible. For example, I identify as a partner, a father, a Chicano, a poet, a teacher, a soccer player, a son, a friend, and on and on. Go back and narrow your list down to five identities that are most important to you (a difficult task I know). Write about the list of five identities and why they are important to you.

Representative Poems

that illustrate identity are:

- o "Foundation" (p. 28)
- o "Crows Hold Grudges for Generations" (p. 43)

Theme: **Kinship relationships**

This collection centers on the complex relationship between a father and son. When it comes to kinship ties, just as there is love, there can also be hurt. Consider the following questions: How do we connect with our loved ones who themselves carry hurt or trauma? How do we reconcile our love for others with the pain they cause? In what ways can we keep hold of loved ones from whom we have been separated?

Prompt:
1. Select a picture of a loved one. Free write about the memories that the image brings up for you, wherever they may go. What feelings does this exercise bring up for you? Choose one memory and write a poem through those feelings.

2. Select a song that reminds you of a loved one. Choose a lyric from the song and write a poem using that line as the title.

Representative Poems

that illustrate kinship relationships are:

Theme: **Loss**

The central theme of this collection is loss: how we navigate it; how we process it; how it becomes part of our journey through life. While the experience of loss is individual, the outside world tells us how to deal with loss, when to feel specific feelings or when and how to move on. Consider the following questions: How has society's expectations of how to grieve shaped your experience of loss? In what ways have society's narratives of loss helped and/or hindered your experience of loss?

Prompt

1. Select a current event where a loss has happened. Explain how you imagine the individuals directly impacted by this event feeling about this loss? Is that different or

similar to how you are experiencing this loss?

2. Select a movie, TV show, YouTube clip that depicts a loss. Write a letter to one of the characters to explain how you feel about their loss.

Representative Poems

that illustrate loss are:

- o "Built to Mourn" (p. 1)
- o "To Dream is to Mourn" (p. 18)
- o "There is a Ghost in my House" (p. 34)

ACKNOWLEDGMENTS

Thank you to the literary journals that gave my poems their first homes: *Iron Horse Literary Review, Quarterly West, Glass' Poets Resist, Dark Marrow, The Oxford Review of Books, PALABRITAS, Homology Lit., the Acentos Review, Puerto del Sol, Into the Void, Lunch Ticket, Rattle's Poets Respond, Apogee Journal, Ghost City Press,* and the wonderful anthology *Puro Chicanx Writers of the 21st Century.*

Thank you to my writing community. All the growth that I have made in my writing practice could not have happened without you. I am particularly grateful to Muriel Leung, Alan Chazaro, Jerry Flores, Marcelo Hernandez Castillo, Preeti Vangani, Jenny Qi, Rosebud Ben-Oni, Jose Hernandez Diaz, and Gustavo Hernandez. Your feedback and support have been invaluable.

Thank you to J. K. Fowler and Laura Salazar for believing in my book and bringing it into existence.

To Raina J. León, your sharp editorial eye and ability to get to the heart of what I am trying to transmit to readers made this collection much stronger. Thank you for validating choices that reflect my authentic self.

To my sister, Yesi, and brother, Alex, thank you for always being there for me. I love you both dearly.

Thank you to my little humans, Romero and Issa, for bringing so much joy into my life and inspiring me to pursue my literary dreams. I hope I make you both proud.

Thank you to my partner, Kati Barahona-López, for being my first reader,

making time and space for my creative work, and being a general badass. You are my role model and every day I strive to be a little more like you. Thank you for navigating life with me. I love you.

Mamá, gracias por darme la vida y por darme la confianza y el apoyo necesario para sobresalir. La quiero muchísimo.

Papá, no pasa un solo día sin que yo piense en usted. Más de una década después de su muerte el dolor sigue allí, evolucionando y persistiendo. Aunque nuestra relación fue compleja nunca he dudado de su amor por mi. Lo quiero y lo extraño tanto.

And finally to you dear reader, thank you for spending time with my rivers.

Gustavo Barahona-López

Gustavo Barahona-López is a writer and educator from Richmond, California. In his writing, Barahona-López draws from his experience growing up as the son of Mexican immigrants. His micro-chapbook 'Where Will the Children Play?' was part of the Ghost City Press 2020 Summer Series. He was a finalist for the 2021 Quarterly West poetry prize. A member of the Writer's Grotto and a VONA alum, Barahona-López's work can be found or is forthcoming in Iron Horse Literary Review, Puerto del Sol, The Acentos Review, Apogee Journal, Hayden's Ferry Review, among other publications.